SILENCE OF THE MORNING

SILENCE
of the
MORNING

Leonard Clark

London
ENITHARMON PRESS
1978

First published in 1977
by the Enitharmon Press
22 Huntingdon Road
East Finchley
London N2 9DU

SBN 0 905289 25 0 (hardbound)
SBN 0 905289 30 7 (paper)

The Enitharmon Press acknowledges assistance
from the Arts Council of Great Britain.

*Printed and made in Great Britain by Skelton's Press, Cannon Place,
Wellingborough Northamptonshire*

I

Walking fields in the silence of the morning,
dazzled by dew, long hedges following me,
I try to recapture the mute man I once was,
before, by some miracle of time, I saw you there
clear as water, fixed in my own geography,
music enfolding us, rising to the arches,
night falling soft outside,
your eyes, live and wondering,
writing warm sounds on the listening air,
and knew, as by alchemy, I had been changed.

I was a man who hid himself,
not daring to venture out to be hurt,
companion of solitude, lonely stars.

And how could you know, my dumb watching there,
I reached out for you then, tattered and cold,
yearning to be invited to sit at your fire,
had come at last to my heart's home?

But now, the birds singing your name,
I walk in the blessing of a new day,
transfigured by you and sunlight,
autumn dropping its blood,
far hills lifted up, and praising,
the fields shining.

II

And I am in your hands,
hands which bless the bread when it is broken,
are lifted up to the glory of the morning,
comfort the slow dying, give
new light to blind eyes.
Held to the shape of a prayer
are stronger than summer leaves
when tempest strikes, soft
as petals of velvet rose,
explore mysteries of water, air.
Hands to hold me close in the warm dark,
speak in words not spoken by lips,
alive with healing, love's fire.

Here are my hands;
with their old stigmata,
they have rejoiced in pebbles,
down of bird, grained wood.
Take them now,
twine our fingers into one stem;
let them become your hands,
burst into tears and flowers.

III

My woods are weeping in the rain,
Their tears are leaves of autumn gold,
But tears of joy and not of pain,
For love gives back a hundredfold.

Your fields are sleeping in the sun
Beneath the hills and peaceful skies,
Their harvest never shall be done,
For love will take them by surprise.

My woods will soon be thick with snow,
Your fields lie deep in winter floods,
And when again your grasses grow,
My woods will have their breaking buds.

The rain will fall, the sun still shine ,
And every word of truth be said,
My woods are yours, your fields are mine,
By love they are inherited.

IV

The moon rising, full into our eyes,
and huge over houses clustered below,
with church tower reduced to a toy,
I followed you in silent climb
through broken and bare trees,
innocently over hidden roots
and spring flowers you knew were there;
I felt them move in me.
Then up and up, beyond the bending copse,
the glad sight of you calling me on,
to reach the top of your familiar hill,
stone, grass and bough your childhood's territory;
it seemed every field was balanced on the sheer slope.
And underneath the soaking turf,
the iron dead huddled up in their long winter.
I watched you on that old ground,
the stillness becoming more still,
and knew, the night witnessing it there,
you had given me your hill,
a free gift in time, no word needed,
but only hand on hand to seal the bond.

And still with slow, remembered tread,
I climb that simple hill to find my peace,
and you, waiting quietly there for me,
beneath a wide embracing sky.

V

Let silence fall
    And beauty bathe your sleeping head,
    Where now, in dream, all troubles gone,
    You have no tears but wait the sun.
    Such beauty that the skies are stilled,
    The earth is trembling, and the stars
    Speak words that only love can hear.

Let silence fall
    That I may wonder that this grace
    Can bring such rapture on this night
    And flood me with your ecstasy.
    For I, deep-drowned in sombre shade,
    Had lost my way, though knew the light
    Was shining near, but not for me.

Let silence fall
    On all that's past and dead as leaves,
    The frost within my bones, the fog,
    For now in loveliness you wake
    To lift your eyes unto the hills,
    Where soon we walk the upper air
    Together in its purity.

VI

Have been home with you,
these ripening days.

The house, waking at morning
to bird song, first shadows on the hill;
in winter, locked by snow, all fields
solid and crisp at evening;
glow of fire, lamplight with music.

History walks these cool rooms,
the churchyard dead wrapped in their turf,
wait for remembering prayers,
you, live and warm, beneath raftered sky,
hearing what strange seas, water or leaves,
beat beyond Eggardon in the still dark.

The years drift with thistledown,
waggons and old singers gone;
smocked ghosts come to sit down with you,
cider and harvest feast, horned lanterns burn
their slow way to cottage and combe;
a coin of Constantine falls
with poetry from Hardy's fingers, Barnes
peers through candleflame at print
waving in thumbed dictionary,
mumbles the Saxon tongue.

The house breathes your silence;
your silence speaks my heart's words.

So it was, when a child,
I moved with my spirit through trees
out of the twilight house,
supper table laid, rosebuds and frost
sparkling in the room, a cat
curled up in soft dream,
mother alone with her dead.

And there at the wood's end,
I stood solitary beneath starlight,
owls calling up the midnight bell,
hoping I might find you there,
to reach for my hand,
you, who had not been born,
nor could ever know until now,
how much I needed you then,
what mystery was stirring in the silence,
nor at what point in time,
I should be waiting for you.

And you eager to come.

VII

I hesitate on the threshold,
tongue-tied and still,
not daring to enter;
a false word, some sudden move,
might shatter the atmosphere,
disturb frail memories.

Your fingers clasp mine in the starred dusk,
whose blessing this room ever is,
pressing their welcome;
"Come in. Here I was born."
I feel the deep significance
as I come to your beginning.

The room itself could be any
in some old, vicarage house,
books, beds, wardrobe, chairs,
evidences of family histories,
a sanctuary for winter guest;
nothing extraordinary,
only your birthday breathing there,
and I, of all visitors, stooping
to see your eyes first open,
inheriting seas and fields,
greeting me, wanderer out of time.

The garden is asleep,
glebe and graves in shadow,
the church tower silent,
wind sighing under the hill,
a bird calling in the dark.

If time could unwind itself,
snow would fall now,
anonymously, unseen,
drift with the hours,
confuse all hedges, block roads,
make an enchanted island of this house;
O, but I feel the flakes falling on me.

There is some revelation here;
I lie at peace in the hopeful dark,
your love fresh on face and hands,
the pangs of birth searching me out.
It is I, taking the shape of your bed.
who am born again, given a new voice.
I am torn from my world's old womb,
neither struggle nor pain,
only love's agony, my glad rejoicing cry.
Lodged in the innocence of your arms
I am baptised all my days,
share the bread with you.

VIII

You in my arms, I,
not believing, turned to tears
you did not see, they did not fall.
Could say no words, none
needed then to seal the bond,
peace with you at last
in silence there, everything known.
Signed with those tears, a pact at will,
out of time, no breaking it now,
witnessed by our secret selves.
Folded together in certainty, as buds
wait to flower, warmed by winter sun,
or leaves opening at first light.
O, but little I have to give in exchange,
so few days to add to the lease,
yet what remains I will to you.
How far we come after the dark
journey of doubts, but yet I know
time will take you out of my days,
love not weaken, but I breathe
it in another air, become
some part of it, and you,
remembering this moment's covenant,
discover me still in its atmosphere.

IX

Working on an old poem late at night,
nothing would come, could not say
what I wanted to say, page after page
scrawled over with sterile graffiti.
I put the thing away, defeated, labour in vain,
angered I had not sized up to the skill,
the foetus still in my head, no separate life.
Came back after sleep with more calm,
craved for release, stared at a blank wall.
Mind wandering, then thought of you
waking with love at sunrise now
somewhere out of my range;
was charged again.

The poem changed shape, flowered at my will,
the seed grew, came to flower, I saw the fruit;
the word made flesh.

A lover in my arms, I was at one with the words,
was with you.
How strange a conception that you at that hour
had delivered my child.

X

On such a night as this,
stars at Verona waited the moon's rising,
summer gardens, perfume and silence,
an orchard drenched with dew fall,
somewhere a lute, chequered olive trees;
a lady, virgin as peach blossom,
looked eternity in the face,
spoke her love to the smooth air.
She gave herself freely, all she was,
flooded with passion, ears tuned to rapture,
not knowing her dark end,
as now, these city skies spitting rain,
fog blinding the eyes of the houses,
skeleton leaves drifting into dank holes,
I give myself to you, all I am,
the full testament of my being,
who am no Romeo,
nor have his burning tongue;
but still, beyond the whisper of the grave,
shall follow you, and them, into infinity,
on such a night as this.

XI

When, sitting at heart's ease together,
we listen to the room's silence, the beat
outside of winter's weather,
our concord is perfect, complete.
We do not need words
to say what each could say,
but know, like sure-winging birds,
our homeward way,
nor, at this gentle mating hour,
love blessing us there,
any music to flow or flower,
but touch of finger, fall of hair,
and eyes which look into eyes
to have a glimpse of paradise.

XII

A smell of beeswax, timber
golden and mellow as honey,
the house lulling the afternoon away,
gone into silence with roses and peaches.
And she who loved me first, all her days,
moving, full-skirted and quiet,
into the legends of sunlight.
I hold the last of her now in my hand,
her tea-cup, green-spotted and fragile,
see my life poured slowly from it
beneath drooping trees, pigeons moaning.

A vision of meadowlands, grasses
vivid and blazing as summer,
the house breathing the evening away,
here still with wood flame and music.
And you who love me last, all my days,
walking, young-eyed and eager
into the gospels of sunlight.
I hold the first of you now in my hands,
your ring, strong-moulded and silver,
see my life begin again from it
beneath singing skies, fields rejoicing.

XIII

Break of day, in waving dream
I heard some fields whispering together,
grass blades bending beneath familiar skies;
it seemed every turf was trembling
with wordless praises.
Hunched hedges joined in the concord,
thorn thicket and bud murmuring,
trees, black and naked, scattered on hillsides
moved humming branches in a bleak wind,
the hills themselves, transported and shaking;
little earthquakes of adoration.
And soon, sleeping birds, fluffed in warm holes,
woke with their chorus, hedgehog and shrew,
to snuffle carols of the damp mould,
every animal drowsy in stable and byre,
bellowing joy to jubilant stars;
the dead stirred in their graves,
birth and resurrection ruffling winding sheets,
the sun rising to a great crescendo.

Every voice was there in adoration,
my head full of the singing.

I cannot tell what mystery was sounding there,
at break of day, that paradisal morning;
I woke to its fading,
but knew, dead of winter, love had been born again,
and earth clamouring for unison with heaven.

XIV

The winter hill, suddenly transfigured by
    out-of-season weather,
waits for first fingers of spring to touch its
    slow-waking slopes,
stands calm sentinel over village, stream
    sparkling below;
and other hills on the far skyline have their
    afternoon shadows.
A few birds, deceived by sunlight, break into singing
in hedges still tight-budded, the long fields are sodden,
grasses seem to grow half-inches before our
    wondering eyes,
flower-heads in the banks secretly uncurl themselves.

This old land turns like a waggon wheel,
    a Sunday peace,
serene with memory, and prospect of lambs
    and early bees,
unified and blessed by love, tongueless,
    but shining.

Face to face, hand in hand, we become
    a breathing unison,
one with the heaving earth, and heaven, shadows
    merging with the sun,
grass bending to grass, flower to flower,
    hills bowing down,
the birds singing one song, the living raising the dead.
A Dante and a Beatrice lodged on English turf,
unfettered by place or time, we have a new identity,
tremble in hope and ecstasy upon the dark verges
    of infinity.

XV

I hold the small and single page in trembling hand,
your letter, reading again at day's slack end,
words seen first by morning's fuzzed eyes,
that through the hours have spoken out loud, over and over,
printing themselves everlastingly on my unbelief.
I did not think it could be, that you,
should declare your simple love for me,
separated from you by so many jealous years,
nor that I might touch you here on this paper's white.
But it is so. I marvel at the miracle.

And now I deliver your affirmation to the fire,
the sacred fire which purifies, does not destroy
but silently changes an old form for a new;
your words remain in the residue, indestructible.

The black and fluttering ashes are no sign of mourning,
nor grief, that time or death shall separate again,
for, phoenix-like, we shall rise up from them,
and meet once more, as on a marriage morning,
redeemed by love, renewed by faith.

I need such holy metamorphosis,
that I may stand before you whole,
wearing the words you wrote
upon quickened ears and eyes,
the fire still burning.

XVI

Washed up by last night's tide into quiet water,
this battered shell, lying alone, unique,
bone-white on littered sand,
brings creation's morning with it,
wave upon wave murmuring in,
my low blood unexpectedly quickening.
This sunlight brightens the rocks,
picks out footprints that are only ours,
and you, caught by chance in its fleeting glow,
take the shell up, cold into your intimate air,
hold to warm lips, gently breathe
what I do not hear, through the milky whorls;
then, turning away from the gull-haunted sea,
give to me, innocently as a child,
my eyes clouding with a cataract of tears,
and see through blurred, revealing gaze,
a million wrinkled years balanced on my palm,
and love fashioned to the shape its first day held,
hear the music of that primeval yesterday,
spiralling round its frail architecture.
It will be whispering still
when we have gone beyond these winter shores
and in some new dimension speak
a language which this shell, with us,
will share and perfectly understand.

XVII

Here where nippled hills bare themselves to the Easter sun,
Hedgerows are all primrose and violet,
I declare my love again to you;
The grasses are a silent witness.
This old land, furrowed and ridged, holds secrets
It shares only with those who come
Quietly at dewfall, or, in recollection,
See, as in ruffled water, sky and valleys rippling.
I declare my love because I must,
Nothing can still it or dam its flood;
And, if suddenly we both broke into primroses,
With violets sprouting at hand, foot and shoulder,
I should not be surprised by such transformation,
But only wonder why all the land did not turn
To flowering, the hills to singing,
The heart's winter never to return,
And the whole earth rising, rising.

XVIII

The light is Dutch light, clear, serene;
the old masters knew it, Ruisdael and Avercamp,
Vermeer at Delft, January afternoons,
spring at sleep in their palette-boxes,
frost hung fresh on muted grass,
vermilion sun folding up over black dykes,
as now it picks out this one field,
flooding it for an hour or so with ochre.
A few hungry birds peck at nothing,
skeleton hedges have short shadows,
a broken harrow rusts away time.

The field is fallow,
lines clean, and waiting,
life working silently beneath the turf;
on either side, plumed kale, veridian,
new furrows, dark as umber.

And lovers, too, have their seasons of fallowness,
when fires are low, yet still are glowing there,
a time to rest, mellow and silent;
waiting secure, in winter's sunlight,
another seeding, a fuller harvest.

The old masters knew it.

XIX

Iron man, speak to me
from your litter of bone and shard,
where now on summer turf I lie alone,
brooding, perplexed,
beneath your graveyard hill,
breathing this valley's unbearable silence.
Speak to me of the frosted days,
the starved tribe huddled together for warmth,
fearful under dumb stars,
horses whinneying in the long dark,
snow levelling the maze of ditches and banks.
Speak,
you who lolled away
the summer minutes in thyme-scented grass,
scabious trembling, cattle
shadowing the carved slopes,
skylarks singing over water and wood below.
How was it with you then?
What unseen terrors clutched at your throat
each fevered night among embers and sling stones,
waiting for the god at morning to shine?
Speak, furred man,
I have no comfort here,
millenials of grief away from you,
no answers to any questions I ask myself
before my tears turn to iron.

Living man, I do not understand,
and did not ever know.
I felt only the wind's blade,
the wild assault of the rain on my skull,
and saw the brooch I made for her,
fading in cold hand,
my eyes remembering.
I met each labyrinthine day as it came,
went to my lonely end.
I took what I could while it was,
gave back what was given me,
held in my tears.
Living man, live,
love on.

XX

The long wood, balanced on the hill's lip
beneath a sky, dun as a trout's back,
sees the weather dotted over sodden meadows.
The wood is littered, needles and cones,
heads of pines block out what light there is.
Walking without words along snaking tracks,
they search for some revelation,
a gospel for the heart.
There is none but spring's green face on buds,
no movement of resurrection;
blinded by winter's cold neutrality,
they have forgotten what light there once was,
how it encircled them.

And then at the tunnel's end,
a single ray breaks through, suddenly,
marrying the meadows to the rising hill,
piercing with laser beam the tangle of undergrowth,
light recovered.

XXI

After the strong climb into the morning sky,
they left the track for the dewed fields,
turned downhill, gulls wheeling above,
over a criss-cross pattern of tractor ruts,
and came to the copse.
She shared the small secret with him,
his head already planted with childhood trees.
Two score of autumns returned for him again,
with beech leaves lying in crinkled layers,
blackberry tangles, rose hips burning,
silver birds on mossed branches.
She moved through the soft stillness,
gathering bracken for the year's ripe festival.
Her arms filled with the huge harvest fronds,
the copse became love's crucible,
she more golden than barley meadows
or sun westering in full radiancy,
he an Inca priest at his glad worshipping.
A new element suddenly discovered there,
the heart's alchemy proven.

XXII

You are my heart's joy: my hope of salvation on earth,
My longed-for shore: my perfect island,
My one and final benediction.
When I ached in my spirit, you comforted me,
Calmed my fears: soothed away my sorrows.
You took my hand: let me to a place of consolation.
I thought I was no man: you reassured me.
You gave me love: I breathe its potency.
Nothing can assail me now: no one tread me down.
You have given me wings: I soar to the heavens.
Your eyes look deep into me: I see love in them.
I hear small leaves whispering in hedgerows,
New corn springing, buds opening.
You are music at midnight, sigh of water on pebbles,
Every shell that sings everlastingly on suncaught beaches.
Shy as mouse at barley time, you are unfettered,
Freer than high clouds floating, snowflakes drifting,
Sweeter than new bread: clear as mountain stream.
I salute you with the glad sound of trumpets,
Speak your name to murmuring grasses,
Write it with my finger in dewfall; it blesses my tongue.
I am made new: the years have dropped from me.
You shall not fade: nor wither into forgetfulness.
You are all the days of my life: my immortality.
And I am your strong protection.

Limited to four hundred
and eighty copies, including
thirty on special paper